D0994330

THE GIRL ON THE SOFA

Jon Fosse

THE GIRL ON THE SOFA

(Jenta i sofaen)

in an English version by David Harrower

from a literal translation by
Neil Howard and Tonje Gotschalksen

OBERON BOOKS
LONDON

First published in English in 2002 by Oberon Books Ltd.
(incorporating Absolute Classics)
521 Caledonian Road, London N7 9RH
Tel: 020 7607 3637 / Fax: 020 7607 3629

e-mail: oberon.books@btinternet.com
www.oberonbooks.com

Jenta i sofaen copyright © Det Norske Samlaget 2002

English version copyright © David Harrower 2002

Jon Fosse is hereby identified as author of this play in accordance with section 77 of the Copyright, Designs and Patents Act 1988. The author has asserted his moral rights.

David Harrower is hereby identified as author of this version in accordance with section 77 of the Copyright, Designs and Patents Act 1988. The author has asserted his moral rights.

All rights whatsoever in this play are strictly reserved and application for performance etc. should be made before commencement of rehearsal to Casarotto Ramsay and Associates Ltd, National House, 60–66 Wardour Street, London W1V 4ND (e-mail: agents@casarotto.uk.com). No performance may be given unless a licence has been obtained, and no alterations may be made in the title or the text of the play without the author's prior written consent.

All rights whatsoever in this version are strictly reserved and application for performance etc. should be made before commencement of rehearsal to Casarotto Ramsay and Associates Ltd, National House, 60–66 Wardour Street, London W1V 4ND (e-mail: agents@casarotto.uk.com). No performance may be given unless a licence has been obtained, and no alterations may be made in the title or the text of the play without the author's prior written consent.

This book is sold subject to the condition that it shall not by way of trade or otherwise be circulated without the publisher's consent in any form of binding or cover other than that in which it is published and without a similar condition including this condition being imposed on any subsequent purchaser.

A catalogue record for this book is available from the British Library.

ISBN: 1 84002 326 0

Cover design: Andrzej Klimowski

Typography: Richard Doust

Printed in Great Britain by Antony Rowe Ltd, Chippenham.

International New Writing and the Traverse Theatre

In 2001 *Jenta i sofaen*, a new play in Norwegian, was commissioned from Jon Fosse by the Traverse Theatre, Scotland. David Harrower's version, *The Girl on the Sofa*, was then commissioned by the Traverse under its international Playwrights in Partnership scheme (in association with the Paul Hamlyn Foundation).

Playwrights in Partnership was created by the Traverse in 2000 as part of the theatre's increased commitment to contemporary international playwrights alongside its development and championing of Scottish writers. The PiP scheme aims to improve the quality of performance translations of contemporary international drama. Each PiP commission matches an international playwright with their Scottish counterpart. The two playwrights are brought together in residency to work on a version of the play into Scots English (if necessary working with a literal translation), and the work's strength to date lies in the extensive involvement of the international playwright in the translation of their own play, paired with the skills of the Scottish partner playwrights as wordsmiths and dramatists.

The Girl on the Sofa was first performed on Monday 12 August 2002 by the Edinburgh International Festival in co-production with the Schaubühne am Lehniner Platz, Berlin.

Characters

WOMAN

GIRL

MAN

MOTHER

SISTER

UNCLE

SISTER OLDER

FATHER OLDER

FATHER

This version of *The Girl on the Sofa* was first performed by the Edinburgh International Festival, in a co-production with the Schaubühne am Lehniner Platz, Berlin, at the Royal Lyceum, Edinburgh, on 12 August 2002. The cast included:

WOMAN, Ruth Lass

MAN, Paul M Meston

GIRL, Abby Ford

MOTHER, Julie Legrand

SISTER, Leah Muller

UNCLE, Daniel Cerqueira

SISTER OLDER, Liz Kettle

FATHER OLDER, Michael Mellinger

Director, Thomas Ostermeier

Designer, Rufus Didwidszus

Large, open, vaguely defined room. The walls made up of loose surfaces, of different sizes. Three of these are large unfinished paintings; the first shows the stern of a ship in turbulent seas; the second a man standing in the middle of a ship (he is much larger than the ship). The third and central painting is of a young girl sitting naked, with her feet drawn up, in the left-hand corner of a sofa. The other surfaces are ordinary walls with family photos, etc.

Behind the surfaces and in between them, in light and in the dark, still or moving, are the WOMAN, the SISTER, the MOTHER and the others.

A table and chairs in the middle, strongly lit.

A WOMAN, around fifty, moves from her place between the surfaces, proceeds hesitantly towards the middle, stops, turns towards the painting of the girl on the sofa, then moves forward, looks again at the painting.

WOMAN

No
(*Short pause.*)
it's so bad
(*Short pause.*)
I can't paint
Nobody's ever said I could of course
(*Short pause.*)
apart from me
so
maybe
I'm not sure
how it happened
(*Short pause.*)
I suppose I was sitting there
yes there on the sofa looking and looking
And then

(*She takes a paintbrush and goes and paints a little on the girl. The GIRL comes in, wearing briefs and shirt, sits in the left-hand corner of the sofa with her feet drawn up. The WOMAN returns to where she was, looks back at the picture.*)
and you have to do something I suppose
When I was a child I'd draw
was good at drawing
But who isn't
Most children are good at drawing

GIRL
I'm quite good at drawing

WOMAN
So I suppose that's what happened
(*Short pause.*)
and so
yes
yes I suppose there was something I had to express
maybe
(*Short pause.*)
I saw a little girl today
she was walking along the road

GIRL
Today
what'm I going to do today

WOMAN
I suppose I wasn't very good at living
But you do live
And so
yes
yes in order to escape
in a way
maybe
yes
yes so I got the idea I should start to paint
And now I've painted
and painted

and painted
all these years

GIRL
I'm so bad at school
But I've a day off
And maybe
maybe I'll go into town

WOMAN
And you have to do something
And the pictures are big
fill room after room
(*Short pause.*)
Some of them I've destroyed
What else could I do
Pictures take up space
They're heavy
They take up all the space
there is
And when there's no space left
yes then you have to do something
with all the pictures
(*The WOMAN puts down the paintbrush, looks at the GIRL sitting on the sofa.*)

GIRL
Maybe I can paint pictures

WOMAN
Ever since I was young
I've painted

GIRL
I'm good at drawing
(*Quite short pause.*)
and maybe I can paint pictures

WOMAN
And
yes

(*Short pause.*)
yes it feels like the pictures
inhabit everything
not because they're good
but because they're pictures
The colours in the pictures
they rise
and they
the colours
(*Short pause.*)
come towards me
now and then
anyway
they scare me
(*Short pause.*)
the colours come out of the picture
and they wrap around me
heavy
clinging
or light
and thin
like water

GIRL
What'm I going to do today

WOMAN
No
(*Short pause.*)
I can't paint
And I've stopped painting so many times
I have
I've stopped and stopped
And then I've started again
Not because it felt right
But you have to do something
And of course I've studied it
I've been learning how to paint
for many years

(*Short pause.*)
And I've
yes
well
I've exhibited in fact
as well
I have
and I've been part of
(*Cuts herself off.*)
yes some things have happened
but not that many
strictly speaking
in relation to everything I've painted
(*Short pause.*)
no
no actually almost nothing's happened
(*Pause.*)
I haven't sold one single picture
well maybe one
maybe
or
yes one picture
maybe
yes a long time ago

GIRL
Why's nothing
the way they say it is

WOMAN
And nobody wants my pictures
And it's easy to understand of course
because I can't paint
so why would anyone want to have
what I paint
(*The WOMAN goes back and looks at the picture.*)
No it's laughable
(*The MAN, around the same age as the WOMAN, comes in and walks towards her.*)

MAN
(*Looks at the picture.*)
It's nice

WOMAN
No
(*Short pause.*)
it's bad
(*Pause.*)

MAN
I had a lot to do today

WOMAN
Yes
(*Short pause.*)

MAN
You don't like the picture

WOMAN
It's
(*Cuts herself off.*)

MAN
(*Continuing.*)
the same as usual

WOMAN
Yes
(*Pause.*)
I can't paint
(*The WOMAN looks towards the MAN.*)
Don't say you know
(*The WOMAN laughs briefly.*)

MAN
No no
(*Pause.*)

WOMAN
But

MAN
Yes

WOMAN
yes today

MAN
Yes

WOMAN
When I was out
out shopping

MAN
Yes

WOMAN
I saw a little girl

MAN
A little girl

WOMAN
Yes
yes I saw a little girl
walking along the road

MAN
Yes

WOMAN
And she was walking so decisively
so purposefully
as if she was afraid
but determined as well
And she had a big rucksack on her back
and the rucksack was half the size of her
almost
anyway
And she had a hat on that was too big for her
She was walking right on the edge of the road
And the cars kept driving and driving past her

And she was walking there right on the edge of the road
She didn't look up
I was walking towards her
And then she saw me
I could tell that she saw me
(*The GIRL looks towards the WOMAN.*)
And then she got scared

MAN
Scared

WOMAN
Yes I could tell she was scared
she was scared because someone was coming towards her
she started to walk more hesitantly
but she walked on
she made herself
(*The GIRL looks down.*)
She knew what she had to do
She walked on
(*Short pause.*)

MAN
(*A little questioning.*)
She was going to school

WOMAN
Yes of course she was going to school
It's a terrible way to go to school
So many cars
yes you know of course
(*The MAN nods. Short pause.*)
I can see her now
Why's it like that
Why do you see something
and then you can't
forget it

MAN
It's just like that
It happens to me too

And maybe
yes maybe it's like that
something one sees
can begin to mean
so much
somehow almost means much more than itself
yes
yes as if God
wants to say something by it
If he exists
(*Short pause.*)
None of that
I shouldn't be saying things like that
Can't you paint her

WOMAN
Then I'd be able to paint
but I can't paint
you know that of course

MAN
Yes and no

WOMAN
I can't paint
but I can see
and that's why
(*Cuts herself off.*)

MAN
Yes that you thought
you could paint

WOMAN
Yes
yes of course that's why
(*Pause.*)
Maybe she reminded me
yes that girl
of myself

when I was small
Or she reminded me
(*Cuts herself off.*)

MAN
Let's not talk about that

WOMAN
No
(*Pause.*)

MAN
I'm tired

WOMAN
Yes
(*Pause. The MAN leaves and the WOMAN looks towards the GIRL.*)

GIRL
And Mother's almost never at home
And my Sister as well
And Father's always away
(*Pause.*)

WOMAN
And now Mother's old
She's going to die soon
(*Short pause.*)
I never had a child
(*Short pause.*)
And I'm getting old myself
(*Short pause. The WOMAN sees the MOTHER come in wearing a dressing gown. The WOMAN picks up a paintbrush, continues painting the GIRL.*)

GIRL
(*To the MOTHER.*)
D'you know where Father is now

MOTHER
(*In her own thoughts.*)
On his ship I suppose

GIRL
When is he coming home

MOTHER
(*Still not completely with it.*)
Could be a long time

GIRL
You don't know

MOTHER
No how am I supposed to know that

GIRL
No

MOTHER
No how am I supposed to
(*Pause.*)
He hardly ever writes
Never telephones
he's out there
on some ship or other
I don't even know where he is
I don't know what the ship's name is

GIRL
He must have written it
(*Short pause.*)
He sends cards
He must have written it
in a card

MOTHER
The name of the ship

GIRL
Yes

MOTHER
Then
I've forgotten it

GIRL
I'm sure you have
(*Short pause.*)

MOTHER
He's been on so many ships

GIRL
He's been at sea for so long

MOTHER
As long as I've known him

GIRL
You married a seaman

MOTHER
I suppose I did

GIRL
D'you regret it

MOTHER
There's no point regretting

GIRL
But do you

MOTHER
Maybe
No what am I saying
Now and then
Maybe

GIRL
And you don't know where his ship is

MOTHER
No
how am I supposed to know that

GIRL
You don't know when he's coming home

MOTHER
No
Can't you talk about something else
(*Short pause.*)

GIRL
Like what
Tell me

MOTHER
Like the weather

GIRL
Like the weather

MOTHER
Yes like the weather

GIRL
It's raining of course like it always does

MOTHER
Not today

GIRL
It's not raining today

MOTHER
Yes it's raining
It's always raining

GIRL
Yes

MOTHER
That's how it is if you're a seaman

GIRL
Yes
(*Pause.*)
It's so long since he was home

MOTHER
Maybe a year
No not as long

half a year
maybe

GIRL
Yes

MOTHER
Yes something like that

GIRL
Yes then he must be coming home soon

MOTHER
Yes I'm sure he is

GIRL
He will

MOTHER
Yes

GIRL
Yes
(*Pause.*)
And when he comes home
he'll have such presents for us
for you and for me
and for my sister

MOTHER
I'm sure he will

GIRL
Bought in a far away country

MOTHER
I'm sure he will have
(*Pause.*)

GIRL
Last time he came
he brought that nice doll with him

MOTHER
Yes it was nice
But a doll
for you
you're almost grown up
(*Short pause.*)
But he doesn't think about that
He still thinks you're a little girl
he yes
in actual fact you're
a grown woman
almost
anyway

GIRL
The doll was nice
it was

MOTHER
But imagine buying you a doll
as if you were a little girl

GIRL
And those nice lamps for the wall

MOTHER
Yes

GIRL
And the nice dresses

MOTHER
Yes
But of course they were
(*Cuts herself off.*)

GIRL
And the large trunk

MOTHER
It's a long time since
he brought that home

(*Short pause.*)
They all do that
they buy trunks
All seamen buy trunks
you know

GIRL
And he made a nice picture-frame

MOTHER
Yes

GIRL
Of empty cigarette packets

MOTHER
Yes

GIRL
Where your wedding picture is now

MOTHER
Yes yes

GIRL
Why do you say that
It's so nice
that picture

MOTHER
Very nice

GIRL
It's so long since the last time
he was home

MOTHER
Yes

GIRL
But he'll be home again soon

MOTHER
I've heard nothing from him

GIRL
You had a card

MOTHER
That was a long time ago

GIRL
Not that long ago

MOTHER
Quite a long time ago

GIRL
Only a week
something like that

MOTHER
A month easily

GIRL
Maybe a month

MOTHER
A month at least
(*Short pause.*)
But
I'd better go

GIRL
Where

MOTHER
I suppose I'll have to go shopping
We have to have food

GIRL
Yes

MOTHER
So I'll go shopping

GIRL
D'you know where my sister is

MOTHER
Asleep I suppose

GIRL
She came home late

MOTHER
I don't know

GIRL
She probably did

MOTHER
Maybe

GIRL
Did you come home late too

MOTHER
Don't ask like that
I'm your mother

GIRL
Yes

MOTHER
Mind your own business

GIRL
I was at home
I was the only one at home

MOTHER
And your sister

GIRL
I don't know where she was

MOTHER
She can't sit at home all the time either

GIRL
No
(*Pause.*)

Today
are you doing anything today

MOTHER
I
(*Cuts herself off.*)

GIRL
Town or anything

MOTHER
Maybe
yes
(*Short pause.*)
maybe I'll meet your uncle

GIRL
Our uncle
again

MOTHER
Maybe

GIRL
Today

MOTHER
Yes that's what I said

GIRL
You meet him nearly every day

MOTHER
He helps so much
we need a man
to help
and father

GIRL
(*Breaking in.*)
Yes

MOTHER
Yes well

GIRL
He may as well live here
Our uncle
(*Short pause.*)
Is he coming here
again today

MOTHER
Stop it now
Maybe
maybe he'll come
we haven't arranged anything
(*The MOTHER leaves. The WOMAN puts down her paintbrush, watches her leave.*)

WOMAN
Father was never there
And Mother
(*Short pause.*)
was out every evening
And Father never came home
And I'd always be sitting there
I'd always sit there
on the sofa

GIRL
I think I want to go into town

WOMAN
And Mother
(*Quite short pause.*)
now she's old
she's ill
she's going to die

GIRL
I can't just sit at home

WOMAN
And Father's dead
And our uncle's dead

GIRL
I think I am good at drawing

WOMAN
More and more often it was our uncle
he came more and more often
and then he was always there
He just was there
(*Short pause.*)
And Father was never there
that doll Father brought with him
I was almost grown up

GIRL
Maybe I can paint pictures

WOMAN
I was almost grown up
And Father came home with a doll
And Mother thought
it was so stupid
And the doll
she looked like
yes like that girl
(*Laughs a little.*)
yes she looked a bit like that girl
that I saw walking to school
Or did she
Maybe she didn't look like her
But I think she did
(*The WOMAN looks around.*)
I'm a bit scared
I'm often scared
I don't know why I'm scared
But I am scared
(*Pause. The MAN comes in.*)

MAN
Are you alright

WOMAN
(*Smiles.*)
Yes thank you

MAN
You mean so much to me

WOMAN
And you mean so much to me

MAN
But you're so unhappy

WOMAN
I'm happy enough

MAN
Yes

WOMAN
It's true
(*Pause.*)

MAN
I have to go now
(*Quite short pause.*)
if I'm to get to work

WOMAN
Yes go

MAN
We'll talk later

WOMAN
Yes
Bye then
(*The MAN goes out and the MOTHER comes in wearing a dressing gown.*)

GIRL
(*To the MOTHER.*)
You aren't dressed yet

MOTHER
There's no rush
You aren't dressed either
so

GIRL
Mother
is my sister up

MOTHER
I don't know
(*Short pause.*)

GIRL
It got so late last night

MOTHER
I told you
I've just woken up

GIRL
Yes I heard
well
(*Short pause.*)
Mother
(*Short pause.*)
Mother

MOTHER
Yes what is it

GIRL
No nothing

MOTHER
Alright

GIRL
But

MOTHER
Yes

GIRL
You
Father
there was a card from him yesterday
Have you seen it
I left it on the kitchen table

MOTHER
Card from Father

GIRL
Yes

MOTHER
Sent from where

GIRL
Lisbon

MOTHER
Yes
well that's good
(*The MOTHER goes out. The GIRL and the WOMAN look towards one another, then the WOMAN turns away. Quite long pause.*)

WOMAN
And I see her before me now
(*Short pause.*)
Is there anything else like that
I remember
No
that's it
I don't think I remember anything else
I remember
(*Short pause.*)
I remember
yes

no it doesn't matter
Why do I remember of all things that Father sent cards
Maybe because it was me
who always got the post
Mother never got the post
for some reason or other she never did
Anyway
there was hardly ever any post
either
That's how it was
Cards from Father now and then
(*Quite short pause.*)
And we'd look at a globe
at where it'd come from
and wonder what the city was like
look at the sea
where the ship he was on
had sailed
those kind of things
But then
then it stopped being fun
Mother hardly looked at the cards he sent
let them just lie
threw them away
maybe
(*The MOTHER comes in, in her dressing gown.*)

GIRL
Will I get the card

MOTHER
If you like

GIRL
It's nice

MOTHER
I'm sure

GIRL
It's nice in Lisbon

MOTHER
The picture's of Lisbon

GIRL
Yes
(*Pause.*)

MOTHER
Your sister must be asleep

GIRL
I think so
(*Short pause.*)
But will

MOTHER
Yes

GIRL
Father
do you think he'll come home soon

MOTHER
What does he say

GIRL
I haven't read the card
it's for you
I don't read other people's post

MOTHER
It's probably for you too

GIRL
Maybe

MOTHER
Oh yes
of course

GIRL
Shall I get it

MOTHER

If you like

(*The GIRL remains seated and the MOTHER goes out. Quite long pause. The WOMAN looks around uncertainly and then moves forward decisively and the MAN enters and he walks after her.*)

MAN

Are you going to leave

(*The WOMAN stops.*)

Are you leaving

WOMAN

Yes

MAN

But

(*Short pause.*)

It would be good to see each other

WOMAN

I want to be on my own

(*Short pause.*)

But when I'm alone

it's good for a while

and then I feel

yes

despondent

it feels

as if no-one cares about me

MAN

But why can't we see each other

WOMAN

When I'm with someone

I want to be alone

My mother

she's ill

she's old

she's going to die

and I don't like her
I've never liked her
And she's never liked me
not from the moment she gave birth to me
She's always hated me
Why do I say things like this
Why do I use these words
What does it mean
when I say these words
What does it mean

MAN
We have to see each other

WOMAN
What does it mean
when I say that she hated me
It means nothing
Those words
Hated
Hated hate

MAN
We can at least see each other
can't we

WOMAN
I can't be with anyone
And I can't be alone
I wasn't able to live with you
That's how it was
(*The MAN turns, goes out.*)
They're there
But I can't be with them
I'm no longer where others are
I'm another place
I'm a place
where no others are
Where nobody is
Where not even I am

And then I think
(*Laughs to herself.*)
yes I think
think and think
I think
yes
yes for example
yes that the only thing that's worth anything
no
no I don't know what's worth anything
Because life's far too short
(*Irritated with herself.*)
Yes that's what I think
that life is short
What does that say
Nothing
It means nothing really
That life's short
it means that life is short
short in relation to what
to eternity
and of course life's too short
in relation to eternity
but then of course everything's too short
isn't it
and then
yes
in a way life is also an eternity
in relation to
yes to this eternity
It's not as eternal
and just as eternal
as everything else
yes
yes then
yes
yes then

(The GIRL gets up and goes and looks at a photograph of herself which is hanging on the wall, together with other family photographs. She then looks at a photo of the FATHER standing on the deck of a ship, she takes the photo down, stands looking at it. The SISTER comes in, in a nightdress, looks towards the GIRL, then goes and sits in an armchair, drawing her feet up beneath her.)

GIRL
(*Half singing.*)
Never ever again
never ever again
where are you father
out there
out there
on all the world's oceans

SISTER
Stop it

GIRL
(*Continues.*)
There on your oceans
out there on your oceans
there on all the world's oceans
there on your oceans

SISTER
Stop it
I said

GIRL
Out there on the mighty ocean
on your mighty oceans

SISTER
Will you stop it

GIRL
I have stopped

SISTER
Where's Mother

GIRL
How should I know

SISTER
You don't know

GIRL
She's not at home

SISTER
Tell me where she is

GIRL
She went out

SISTER
(*Questioning.*)
went out

GIRL
Yes out

SISTER
And you haven't seen her since

GIRL
No

SISTER
Is it long since she left

GIRL
Yes

SISTER
And she wasn't home last night

GIRL
I don't know

SISTER
You do know

GIRL
I went to bed

SISTER
But she wasn't at home when you went to bed

GIRL
I don't think so

SISTER
No of course she wasn't

GIRL
Where was she then

SISTER
How would I know

GIRL
Don't you

SISTER
No I don't

GIRL
She was probably with her lover I suppose

SISTER
Don't say things like that
She doesn't have a lover

GIRL
How do you know

SISTER
How can I know

GIRL
Why say it then

SISTER
I'm just saying it I suppose

GIRL
You don't know anything about it

SISTER
Yes

GIRL
No

SISTER
Yes

GIRL
What then

SISTER
Women need men

GIRL
She has a man

SISTER
But he's never home

GIRL
No

SISTER
Then does she have a man

GIRL
She has a man
and he
her man
is a seaman
and he's out there on all the world's oceans
(*Short pause.*)
and then he comes home
he comes home to her
to you
to me
to his women
he comes home
and he brings with him
such nice things

SISTER
He's coming home
when's he coming home

GIRL
He's coming home
Of course he must be
he sent a card
not so long ago

SISTER
He's hardly ever home
and he's got
a woman in every port
that's how it is
that's how it is when you're a seaman
seamen have women in every port
you must know that

GIRL
No

SISTER
Everyone says that

GIRL
Yes

SISTER
They say that seamen go to whores

GIRL
Yes

SISTER
They do

GIRL
D'you believe
father goes to whores

SISTER
No

GIRL
Yes you do
You're just saying you don't

SISTER
Then I do I suppose

GIRL
You're mad
Imagine thinking that
I'd have thought
(*Cuts herself off.*)

SISTER
Yes

GIRL
No nothing

SISTER
Say it

GIRL
No nothing

SISTER
Say it

GIRL
No

SISTER
I know what you were going to say

GIRL
Yes

SISTER
That I
Yes I'm a bit of a whore myself

GIRL
No

SISTER
Don't lie

GIRL
Where were you last night

SISTER
Why are you asking that

GIRL
Just asking

SISTER
I was out

GIRL
But you came home so late

SISTER
Yes
aren't I allowed
what's it got to do with you
I come home when I want
I decide myself
You've got nothing to do with it

GIRL
No

SISTER
So why do you ask

GIRL
Nothing

SISTER
Yes
(*Short pause.*)
just say it

GIRL
Those clothes

SISTER
Clothes

GIRL
Yes those clothes

SISTER
What clothes

GIRL
You know which clothes I mean

SISTER
I don't

GIRL
Yes

SISTER
No
(*Pause.*)

GIRL
You do know
(*Pause.*)
Those
(*Short pause.*)
those black ones

SISTER
Have you been looking in my cupboard

GIRL
No

SISTER
Yes

GIRL
No I haven't

SISTER
You have
(*Short pause.*)
You mean the stockings
Those black stockings and the other things

GIRL
Yes
(*Short pause.*)

can I
try them
(*Quite short pause.*)
They look so
(*Cuts herself off.*)

SISTER
Stop it now

GIRL
And that sort of suspender belt thing
and the bra

SISTER
You've been looking in my cupboard

GIRL
Where did you get them from

SISTER
Bought them of course

GIRL
Do you use them

SISTER
I might

GIRL
When do you

SISTER
Don't ask so much

GIRL
I'm just wondering

SISTER
You're always wondering

GIRL
Is that so strange
is it

(*Pause.*)
D'you know where mother is

SISTER
No I've said

GIRL
You didn't say

SISTER
I think she's out
doing something or other
I suppose she's doing something

GIRL
I was just asking
(*Pause.*)

SISTER
Were you at home yesterday

GIRL
Yes
(*Pause.*)

SISTER
Was our uncle here

GIRL
Yes

SISTER
A long time

GIRL
Yes
(*Short pause.*)
I went to bed
so I don't really know
(*Short pause.*)
But he would've been gone when you came home
tell me where you were

SISTER
D'you have to know everything

GIRL
And you were wearing
(*Cuts herself off.*)

SISTER
You have to stop looking in my cupboard

GIRL
I haven't been looking

SISTER
How d'you know then

GIRL
How could I know
(*Short pause.*)
Why did you ask about our uncle

SISTER
I didn't ask about him

GIRL
No

SISTER
I think he was here last night

GIRL
No

SISTER
His shoes
his coat
were in the hall

GIRL
Maybe
(*Short pause.*)
He is our uncle

SISTER
Yes
(*Pause.*)

GIRL
Can I try
(*Cuts herself off.*)

SISTER
No

GIRL
It's always no to me

SISTER
Yes
maybe
another time

GIRL
Now
Straight away

SISTER
No stop it

GIRL
Yes
Where are they

SISTER
In my room
of course

GIRL
You'll let me try them
then

SISTER
No
some other time
not now

GIRL
Yes

SISTER
You who won't even
tell me where Mother is

GIRL
What do you think

SISTER
I suppose she's gone shopping

GIRL
Yes maybe
(*Short pause.*)
or maybe she didn't come home last night
that could've happened

SISTER
And so it was only our uncle who was here

GIRL
It could've been
How would I know
(*Pause.*)
Aren't you going to get dressed soon

SISTER
Stop going on at me
You aren't even dressed yourself yet

GIRL
I'm not going on at you
I just asked

SISTER
Of course you're always
just asking
(*Pause.*)

GIRL
And what about him

SISTER
D'you have to start going on about him too
(*Pause.*)
Who do you mean anyway

GIRL
You must know

SISTER
Yes

GIRL
Yes him

SISTER
I don't understand what you're talking about

GIRL
Yes him

SISTER
Yes
(*Pause.*)

GIRL
Alright
I won't ask any more
I can't say anything
because whatever I say
is wrong
I can't say a single word
You always have to shout at me
And you've done that
since I was born
Mother told me that
that when I was little
before I could talk
or anything
when I was just lying there
you shouted at me then
said

No no
Naughty naughty
Bad girl
Even if I was just crawling around on the floor

SISTER
(*Cuts her off.*)
Yes yes

GIRL
(*Continues.*)
yes you shouted at me
you've never liked me
You've always thought I was just a nuisance
And I'm

SISTER
Not listening

GIRL
(*Continues.*)
I'm
your sister

SISTER
Stop it

GIRL
And you
you dress yourself up in those whore's stockings
there
And you think you look so gorgeous

SISTER
Stop it

GIRL
You put on make-up
until it runs
down your face
And then you walk around in those stockings there
With that black suspender belt

It looks so stupid
And if men

SISTER
(*Cuts her off.*)
What d'you know about men

GIRL
(*Continues.*)
if they think it's

SISTER
(*Cuts her off.*)
Don't talk about men

GIRL
No you're the one who can talk about them
(*Pause.*)
But
yes those clothes
yes
can I
(*Cuts herself off.*)

SISTER
If you want to so much
Yes alright then

GIRL
I want to
(*Pause.*)
can I

SISTER
Now straightaway

GIRL
Yes
can I

SISTER
I'll get no peace if you don't
alright

GIRL
Will you get them

SISTER
I suppose I'll have to
(*The SISTER goes out, the GIRL puts the photo back. Pause. The WOMAN and the GIRL look at each other. Pause. The SISTER enters with a bundle of clothes.*)
Here they are

GIRL
Let's see

SISTER
All yours
(*The SISTER lays the clothes on the table and the GIRL begins to pick them up. First, a pair of black net stockings.*)

GIRL
These stockings
where did you get them

SISTER
Oh it's easy

GIRL
But where

SISTER
They sell them everywhere

GIRL
Not these
they can't

SISTER
Yes
just about

GIRL
No

SISTER
Don't keep saying that
Try them
put them on

GIRL
I don't know if I can

SISTER
It was you who wanted to
(*The GIRL picks up the suspender belt, holds it up in front of her.*)

GIRL
How can you wear things like this
(*The GIRL picks up the bra.*)
Completely see-through

SISTER
Your tits are too small

GIRL
Maybe

SISTER
But you can try if you want

GIRL
I don't think I do

SISTER
No alright
Alright then
Forget it
(*The GIRL picks up the short red patent leather skirt.*)

GIRL
God so sexy

SISTER
Stop it

GIRL
You can't go around in a skirt like that

SISTER
Yes I can

GIRL
No

SISTER
Yes

GIRL
No

SISTER
I can
because I do
You going to try them
or not

GIRL
Not when you're watching

SISTER
Don't be silly

GIRL
Alright then
(*The GIRL begins to pull on a stocking, she pulls on the second. The SISTER stands and watches her, grins.*)
What is it

SISTER
Your knickers are ugly
Yes
They're completely wrong
Maybe you should try mine too
(*The GIRL puts on the suspender belt, tries to fasten the stockings.*)
I'll help you

(*The SISTER fastens the stockings to the suspender belt, takes a position and looks at the GIRL.*)
Oh yes now you're gorgeous
ha
(*The SISTER picks up the bra, holds it out.*)

GIRL
No
it's far too big

SISTER
Try it

GIRL
(*Takes it.*)
Alright then
(*The GIRL takes off her blouse and puts on the bra, it's far too big.*)

SISTER
Yes now you're gorgeous
ha
so gorgeous

GIRL
Don't be silly

SISTER
I'll get some make-up
(*The SISTER hurries out and the GIRL poses, pulls the briefs up further, tries to be as stylish as she can, then she takes the patent leather skirt, pulls it on. The WOMAN looks towards the GIRL, then looks down. The SISTER enters, carrying the doll the FATHER brought, holds it out to the GIRL.*)

GIRL
No

SISTER
Yes
you need to have the doll

GIRL
Don't mess around

SISTER
Yes
(*The GIRL takes the doll.*)

GIRL
I can't stand like this with a doll

SISTER
Sit down
(*The GIRL sits down with the doll in her lap and the SISTER begins to make her up, she makes up her mouth completely red, looks at her.*)
You're becoming completely irresistible now

GIRL
Don't say that

SISTER
And then we have to
(*Cuts herself off, begins to put colour on her eyelashes.*)
Like that yes
Let's have a look at you
Get up
(*The GIRL moves as if to put down the doll.*)
No you have to keep hold of the doll
you must understand that
you're my little sister aren't you
maybe

GIRL
No

SISTER
Yes
(*The GIRL gets up, stands there with the doll under her arm.*)
Go and look at yourself in the mirror
You're a real sight
(*The doorbell rings.*)

GIRL
(*Scared.*)
Somebody's here
You go
I have to take these clothes off
(*The SISTER goes out and the GIRL picks up her blouse and she and the WOMAN look towards each other and the SISTER comes back in.*)

SISTER
Hurry
He's coming

GIRL
Who

SISTER
Our uncle
of course
(*The GIRL hurries out and the SISTER begins to collect up her make-up gear and the UNCLE enters.*)

UNCLE
You're putting your make-up on

SISTER
Yes
Yes I should tidy up a bit
(*Pause.*)

UNCLE
Your mother's not home

SISTER
She's out shopping I suppose

UNCLE
Yes
And you're not dressed yet

SISTER
No
as you can see

UNCLE
Yes
(*Short pause.*)
yes I mean
it's late in the day
already

SISTER
Yes
(*Pause.*)

UNCLE
It's a while since I've seen you

SISTER
I guess

UNCLE
A few weeks
maybe

SISTER
Yes maybe a few weeks

UNCLE
Maybe longer
And everything's alright with you
(*Short pause.*)

SISTER
Yes

UNCLE
Good to hear

SISTER
Mother'll be coming soon
(*Short pause.*)

UNCLE
Have you heard anything from your father

SISTER
No
nothing

UNCLE
Not a thing

SISTER
No
(*Short pause.*)
It's a long time since he sent a card
He used to always send cards

UNCLE
Yes

SISTER
Must be several months since last time

UNCLE
Do you know where he is

SISTER
No

UNCLE
I see
(*The MOTHER comes in, wearing a coat, carrying two shopping bags.*)

MOTHER
(*To the UNCLE.*)
You're here

UNCLE
Yes
(*Pause.*)
yes shouldn't I be

MOTHER
yes of course
It's just so unexpected
in a way

(*The MOTHER looks towards the SISTER.*)
It's late
And you're not dressed yet
You can't go around like that

SISTER
No
(*Pause.*)

MOTHER
So go and get dressed then
(*The SISTER goes out and the MOTHER puts down the two shopping bags, she looks towards the UNCLE who goes over to her and puts his arms round her, she put her arms round him, they kiss. They sit on the sofa.*)
Oof yes

UNCLE
Maybe I shouldn't have come up here

MOTHER
Yes
Of course you should
(*The MOTHER leans against him and he kisses her again, she frees herself from him.*)
But
yes
yes she's home

UNCLE
She'll be getting dressed

MOTHER
Hope so
(*Long pause.*)
I'll take the shopping into the kitchen I suppose

UNCLE
Yes
but I can do it

MOTHER
No you sit
(*The GIRL comes in, in trousers and blouse.*)
You're home too

GIRL
I told you
I'm off school today

MOTHER
Yes maybe you did
(*The MOTHER looks towards the UNCLE.*)
Yes I forget almost everything

UNCLE
(*To the GIRL.*)
Yes
yes your mother needs a bit of help
with something
yes
so here I am
yes

GIRL
Yes
(*Short pause.*)

MOTHER
What do you look like
you've got make-up on

GIRL
Yes

MOTHER
You look terrible
(*The MOTHER gets up and the UNCLE gets up and takes the shopping bags and goes out.*)
Take that make-up off

GIRL
Yes

MOTHER
Yes
(*Pause.*)
What are you going to do today
now that you're off school
I mean

GIRL
I'm not sure

MOTHER
But why've you got so much make-up on

GIRL
I just put it on

MOTHER
Yes
(*Pause.*)
what're you going to do today
you didn't answer

GIRL
Go into town maybe

MOTHER
You should

GIRL
I think I will
(*The MOTHER goes out. Pause. The GIRL sits up in the corner of the sofa with her feet drawn up. Quite long pause.*)

WOMAN
I paint
stupid pictures
I paint a picture of a girl on a sofa
And it becomes only a picture of the girl on the sofa
neither more nor less
Nothing else
Because I can't paint
(*Pause.*)

I haven't painted one good picture in the whole of my life
(*Short pause.*)
And it's true
(*Short pause.*)
because the most significant
insignificance
is always lacking

GIRL
I can't just stay home
I must do something
go into town
maybe

WOMAN
Now I'm trying to paint
a picture of a girl on a sofa
(*The WOMAN looks towards the GIRL.*)
and all it becomes is just
a picture of the girl on the sofa

GIRL
I'm good at drawing
Maybe I can paint pictures

WOMAN
I can't paint
(*Short pause.*)
because I paint only what I see
(*Pause.*)
But life can't be seen
(*Pause.*)
And those who can paint
they paint
(*Quite short pause.*)
yes the invisible
which is life
they paint life
where it disappears

(*Short pause.*)
and emerges

GIRL
And our uncle's always here
And Father's never here
And my sister's at work
and then she goes out
in the evening

WOMAN
I can't paint
(*Short pause.*)
And now I've grown old
or almost old
And my sister's grown old too
And she's got herself a man and children
And a nice house

GIRL
I have to find something to do

WOMAN
And my sister's fine
(*Short pause.*)
And everything that's happened
is still present

GIRL
All I do is
sit here on the sofa

WOMAN
I just talk
I shouldn't open my mouth
(*Short pause.*)
But it's a bit like that
nevertheless
That everything that's been
is still present
without it being there

GIRL

I must want something
But I'm so bad at school

WOMAN

I always say
something or other
which is meant to sound
good
(*Short pause.*)
like the pictures too
in a way
should look good
so good
so nice
All it is is just colours
clinging colours
a heavy thing
amongst other heavy things
All the pictures I've painted
How heavy they are
Heavy from the colours
I'm not even able to move them
All they are is weight

GIRL

I think I'll go into town today
I'm off school

WOMAN

The pictures are just things
heavy things
which must be thrown away
since no-one wants
what I paint
(*Quite short pause.*)
They don't have the space
(*Quite short pause.*)
The pictures are too big

GIRL
I'm good at drawing
Maybe I can paint pictures

WOMAN
I paint badly
I can't paint
(*Pause.*)
I want to paint Mother out

GIRL
(*Looks at the WOMAN, questioning.*)
Paint Mother out

WOMAN
(*Looks at the GIRL, then looks away.*)
I want to paint Mother out
(*Short pause.*)
because of course she wants everything to be so good
And of course I want everything to be so good
like Mother always wanted it to be
everything to be so good
light and easy
like a sunny summer's day
yellow and white
nice
That's how it was to be
light
and yellow and nice and light and easy
And pink
And lace trim
And black

GIRL
I can't just sit here

WOMAN
And yellow
most of all yellow
she wanted it to be

yellow
yellow as the sun
Nothing else
just yellow
(*Short pause.*)
And Mother would walk around
in a pink nightdress
her breasts moving from side to side
how could Father stand it

GIRL
Father's never at home

WOMAN
He couldn't stand it
either
he travelled
or he didn't come home
he stayed out there at sea
on the ocean
or wherever he was
the seaman
He came home
stayed a while
and then he was off again
disappeared
Out the door
And that was him gone

GIRL
I can't just sit here
(*Short pause.*)

WOMAN
There's nothing more to remember
I'm sure
there's nothing more I really want to remember
(*Hesitates.*)
Everything I say
isn't worth saying

GIRL
I think I'll go into town

WOMAN
And what I say
of course means nothing

GIRL
I can't just stay here
(*The SISTER comes in, dressed in net stockings and the patent leather skirt, high-heeled boots. To the SISTER.*)
You've dressed up

SISTER
Yes

GIRL
Have you got all of it on
(*The WOMAN picks up a paintbrush, begins to paint a black suspender belt on the GIRL.*)

SISTER
Yes

GIRL
Everything
the suspender belt too

SISTER
Yes

GIRL
I don't believe it

SISTER
You want to see

GIRL
No

SISTER
Yes you do

(*The SISTER loosens the leather skirt and it falls to the floor and stands there in the net stockings held up with a suspender belt.*)

GIRL
You look like a whore

SISTER
Men like it

GIRL
Yes that's why
Have you got the see-through bra on

SISTER
Yes
(*The SISTER unbuttons her blouse.*)

GIRL
Stop it

SISTER
Didn't you have it on earlier

GIRL
Yes

SISTER
Yes exactly

GIRL
Where are you going

SISTER
Wouldn't you like to know

GIRL
No
(*Short pause.*)
Are you going to meet someone

SISTER
I suppose I am

GIRL
A man

SISTER
I suppose I am

GIRL
Do you
(*Short pause.*)
when
do you do dirty things together

SISTER
Wouldn't you like to know

GIRL
Where are you going to meet him

SISTER
He's picking me up

GIRL
He has a car

SISTER
Yes

GIRL
Do you do dirty things in his car

SISTER
Stop asking me
(*The SISTER pulls up the patent leather skirt, does it up.*)

GIRL
I think you do dirty things

SISTER
Maybe

GIRL
In his car

SISTER

I wouldn't think about it too much
(*The SISTER does up her blouse.*)
I'm going

GIRL

Yes

SISTER

Bye
(*The SISTER goes, stops suddenly and stands looking at the SISTER OLDER, who enters walking towards her and who walks on further towards the WOMAN, who sees her coming, but pretends that she doesn't, plays ignorant, while the SISTER goes out, goes away from the picture and from the SISTER OLDER.*)

SISTER OLDER

(*To the WOMAN.*)
We were going to go together and visit Mother
And you didn't come

WOMAN

(*Stops, turns to the SISTER OLDER.*)
No

SISTER OLDER

We agreed to meet each other
at the Nursing home
we were going to visit her
(*The WOMAN goes towards the picture of the girl on the sofa, as if she's unaware that the SISTER OLDER is talking to her, begins to paint black net stockings on the GIRL.*)
We did didn't we
Today
we were going to go today
You and me
We're sisters aren't we
We're her daughters
The only thing she has in life

(*Short pause.*)
I've been there several times
and visited her
but you
it's such a long time since you've been there
You must come
you have to
for Mother's sake
She's sick
she may die
why don't you like her
why've you never liked her
but now
now Mother is sick
(*Short pause.*)
can't you make your peace with her
you should do it
(*Short pause.*)
before it's too late
(*The WOMAN walks back and stands and looks at the picture, then turns, looks round and stands looking at the FATHER OLDER, who comes walking towards her.*)

WOMAN
Father
it's so good to see you again
I hardly ever see you

FATHER OLDER
Well you know
I'm not well
And I prefer to stay at home

WOMAN
Some home
(*Cuts herself off.*)

FATHER OLDER
It's alright
there

WOMAN
You never complain

FATHER OLDER
It doesn't help hato complain
(*Pause.*)
You're alright

WOMAN
Yes
I suppose I am
(*Pause.*)

FATHER OLDER
You and him
you haven't moved back in together

WOMAN
No
It's better for me to be alone

FATHER OLDER
I can understand that
yes

WOMAN
You'd know

FATHER OLDER
I suppose I do

WOMAN
Yes
(*The FATHER OLDER looks down, goes into himself, then leaves. The WOMAN puts down her paintbrush. Pause. The SISTER OLDER and the WOMAN look towards each other. Long pause.*)

SISTER OLDER
(*Hesitant.*)
But
when Father was alive

while he was alive
you went and visited him
That's how it always was
you and Father
and me and Mother
How did it get like that

WOMAN
Mother never liked me

SISTER OLDER
It was you who didn't like her
That's what you're always saying

WOMAN
But it's true

SISTER OLDER
It's not true
She liked you
And besides
yes
now she's old
she might die any day

WOMAN
Mother never liked me
I liked her
all my life I liked her
from the time I was born
I liked her so much
and I did everything I could
to make her like me
Everything
I
Yes
Everything
(*Short pause.*)
But she didn't like me
And then

yes
it went on so long
I just stopped trying

SISTER OLDER
And you stopped visiting her

WOMAN
Yes

SISTER OLDER
There were so many years
when you hardly saw each other

WOMAN
I didn't want to see her

SISTER OLDER
But you visited Father

WOMAN
Yes yes
yes Father and me
yes
he had no-one else
He sat there in his room
at that Seaman's home
sat there alone
he had almost nothing
he sat there and rolled his cigarettes
went to that dingy café
and drank a few glasses of beer
went back to his room
It was only me who visited him

SISTER OLDER
I couldn't stand seeing him sitting there
His stubble
the smell of smoke
He hardly ever washed himself
(*Laughs briefly.*)

didn't wash himself
or his room
And those yellow brown fingers
Roll-ups the whole time
And if he said anything
yes it was always the same
the same things about the different ships
he'd been on
and said something
something about how he'd met someone or other
who he'd been on a ship with
at some time or another

WOMAN
Yes

SISTER OLDER
He went with whores
I'm sure about that

WOMAN
He was your Father

SISTER OLDER
I'm sure he was

WOMAN
You don't think he was

SISTER OLDER
I'm sure he was my Father

WOMAN
You look like him

SISTER OLDER
Maybe a bit
(*Short pause.*)
You're not coming to see Mother

WOMAN
No

SISTER OLDER
But it's true
she's in a bad way
they rang from the Nursing home
she
yes
yes they asked me to come
you must come

WOMAN
She doesn't like me
It's best
for her
that I don't come

SISTER OLDER
She likes you
She always asks after you
She misses you
I know she does
And now
(*Short pause.*)
yes you
you're going to regret it
if she dies now
Yes
yes I know it
For your own sake you have to come with me
She likes you
She always has
You just misunderstand

WOMAN
You've said that before

SISTER OLDER
It's true

WOMAN
She's never

SISTER OLDER
(*Cuts her off.*)
Stop it
It's not the time for it
We have to go
They rang from the nursing home
Mother isn't well
we have to go
we can't stand here like this
I have to go there
whatever happens
And you should come too
We should go together
We're her daughters
We're all she has
She's alone
She's going to die
We have to go

WOMAN
I don't want to
I'm not going to

SISTER OLDER
You have to

WOMAN
She left me
And I left her

SISTER OLDER
You keep saying that
Mother
(*Hesitates.*)
what was she supposed to do
There was nothing else she could do

WOMAN
No
maybe not

You go
You should go
She
(*Cuts herself off.*)

SISTER OLDER
I don't understand you

WOMAN
Go now

SISTER OLDER
Alright
(*Short pause.*)
But you're going to regret it
I know it
You don't know what you're doing
It's your decision
(*The SISTER OLDER goes out and the WOMAN goes over to the picture of the girl on the sofa, looks at it, then turns and sees the MOTHER come in, dressed in skirt and blouse, and then the UNCLE comes in after her.*)

UNCLE
You're looking lovely

MOTHER
Do you think so

UNCLE
Yes very nice

MOTHER
Thank you

UNCLE
You look so nice
that I
yes I
(*The UNCLE goes over and puts his arms around the MOTHER from behind and presses her against him, he kisses her on the cheek, she turns, they kiss each other a long time.*)

I get so
I start to
Can't we
yes
now
yes straight away

MOTHER
But we can't
(*Cuts herself off.*)
They could be
(*Cuts herself off.*)

UNCLE
They're not at home
Let's do it
Here
On the floor

MOTHER
No

UNCLE
Yes
(*The UNCLE feels her breasts, first over her blouse, then he puts his hands underneath it.*)
Now
I want you
Now
Straight away

MOTHER
But what if

UNCLE
No-one's home
(*Short pause.*)
Or we
yes
yes we can go into the bathroom

MOTHER
Maybe
(*The UNCLE kisses her. The MOTHER frees herself.*)
No we can't
It's morning
Not now

UNCLE
But

MOTHER
(*As if talking strictly to a child.*)
No no
Later
not now

UNCLE
(*A little put out.*)
Alright
(*Pause.*)
Is he coming back soon

MOTHER
I think so
Or maybe not
(*Short pause.*)
I just got a card from him

UNCLE
Yes from some place or other

MOTHER
Yes I don't remember

UNCLE
It's a long time since he was last home

MOTHER
A couple of years
no not so long
I
(*Laughs briefly.*)

no I don't remember
(*The MOTHER kisses the UNCLE on the cheek.*)

UNCLE
But he's coming home soon

MOTHER
Yes he has to

UNCLE
And what then

MOTHER
I've no idea
(*Short pause.*)
why do you have to be his brother
It makes everything so much worse

UNCLE
I can't help it
that's what I am
There's nothing we can do about it
that's how it's turned out
(*Pause.*)

MOTHER
Yes
(*Pause.*)
Should I write to him
about us

UNCLE
No you mustn't
You can't
No not that
It
(*Cuts himself off.*)
No
(*Pause. The GIRL gets up from the sofa where she's been sitting the whole time and walks out on to the floor.*)

MOTHER
(*To the GIRL.*)
You're not at school

GIRL
I'm off
I said that
I told you

UNCLE
(*To the GIRL.*)
Hello

GIRL
Hello

MOTHER
And you
what're you doing today

GIRL
I don't know

MOTHER
You're not playing truant I hope

GIRL
Why d'you say that
I told you I've got the day off
I do get days off school

MOTHER
Yes I didn't mean it that way
(*Short pause.*)
and actually
when I think about it
you did tell me
you did say you'd the day off today
(*Laughs briefly.*)
I don't remember anything
but
yes

UNCLE
Yes she did say that
I remember
She did say she'd have the day off today
that's right

GIRL
I'm going for a walk
into town

MOTHER
Yes do
And your Sister

GIRL
At work
(*The MOTHER and the UNCLE sit on the sofa, and the GIRL goes over to the WOMAN, takes a position next to her. Quite long pause. The UNCLE puts his arm around the MOTHER's shoulders. Pause.*)

MOTHER
Why doesn't he write
letters
I mean
or ring
Just those cards

UNCLE
He's always been like that

MOTHER
Always

UNCLE
Yes

MOTHER
You know him better
than me

UNCLE
Yes and no

MOTHER
You grew up together
you and him

UNCLE
Yes we did
Can't deny that

MOTHER
You were never good friends

UNCLE
No
(*Pause.*)

MOTHER
I suppose brothers
don't always have to be good friends

UNCLE
It can happen
(*Pause.*)
How long's it been since you heard from him

MOTHER
I'm not sure

UNCLE
I suppose he'll send a card
soon
you'll see

MOTHER
Yes

UNCLE
And he'll phone one day

MOTHER
I suppose he might
(*The MOTHER laughs briefly.*)

UNCLE
That's how it is
for a seaman

You know
yes you can't think about too much
about those back home
it can be painful
that
those who think too much about their wife and children
they can't settle
they can't sleep
they sit and stare
at the waves
on the ocean
they can't cope
they begin to drink too much
they get scared
of being alone
that they'll lose their sanity
and jump into the ocean
yes it happens a lot

MOTHER
Don't talk like that

UNCLE
It happens
It's not uncommon
In the dark night
as the ship works and works its way forward
over the black ocean
under the black sky
they go out
and stand in the darkness
holding onto the rail
And between the man standing there
and the enormous darkness
is only that rail
some rusting iron pipes welded together
painted white

MOTHER
You can't say this
Think about us
about me

UNCLE
And the engine which keeps turning

MOTHER
(*Continues.*)
think about us at home
yes about us
what about us
It's not so easy for us
either

UNCLE
No
But he has to
I'm just trying to say that he
he can't think about you too often
that's how it is with a seaman
to be out there on all the world's oceans
to have to stay there
to have to do your work
Then to have to come home again
to the wife
to the children
to the daughters

MOTHER
After having had
a woman in every port

UNCLE
Yes

MOTHER
You think so

UNCLE
That's what it's like

MOTHER
Are you sure

UNCLE
They say that
that it's like that

MOTHER
But what about me

UNCLE
You

MOTHER
Yes
while he
in every port
so I sit
at home
trying to bring up two daughters
the best I can
and then he's doing
yes
(*Cuts herself off.*)

UNCLE
Don't think about it
You shouldn't think about
There's so much in life you shouldn't see
And so much
you shouldn't think about
if you're to cope
so

MOTHER
I can't let it go

UNCLE
No

MOTHER
I can't cope with it
And I
am I not a beautiful woman
(*Laughs a little, and puts it on a bit.*)
attractive
just look
yes even though I've almost full-grown
daughters

MOTHER
am I not
yes quite
yes attractive

UNCLE
You are

MOTHER
But look

UNCLE
Yes

MOTHER
Aren't I

UNCLE
Yes

MOTHER
And I'm here just wasting away

UNCLE
You're looking after your daughters

MOTHER
They're almost grown up

UNCLE
You've got two lovely daughters

MOTHER
You think so

UNCLE
Yes

MOTHER
Yes
(*Pause.*)

UNCLE
And he sends money

MOTHER
Money comes every month

UNCLE
You don't do too
(*Cuts himself off.*)

MOTHER
I don't do too well either

UNCLE
Well who does

MOTHER
No that's true

UNCLE
Yes
(*Pause.*)

MOTHER
You're alright

UNCLE
Getting by

MOTHER
It's the same for you
as

UNCLE

(*Cuts in.*)

Yes

(*The UNCLE puts his arms around her, kisses her and they lie on the sofa, lie and hold each other. Short pause. The WOMAN sees the FATHER OLDER come in and walks towards him.*)

WOMAN

Father

It's so good to see you

But you look

You should

(*Cuts herself off.*)

No I won't say anything

It's good to see you

It's nice you've come

FATHER OLDER

Yes thanks for phoning

and asking me

WOMAN

We hardly ever see each other

FATHER OLDER

Yes

you're right

(*The MAN comes in. The FATHER OLDER moves away from the WOMAN, takes a position, looks down.*)

MAN

(*To the WOMAN.*)

I have to talk to you

WOMAN

It's no good talking

MAN

I need you

WOMAN
It's no good
We've talked and talked
(*Short pause.*)
There's nothing more to say

MAN
Just talk with me

WOMAN
There's nothing more to say

MAN
No

WOMAN
Everything's been said

MAN
But

WOMAN
There's nothing more to say

MAN
What have I done wrong

WOMAN
It's not like that

MAN
What is it
(*Short pause.*)
When I grew up

WOMAN
(*Cuts him off.*)
Yes I know
You've told me so many times

MAN
D'you want me to leave
(*The WOMAN shrugs her shoulders. Pause.*)

WOMAN
You haven't done anything wrong

MAN
But you don't want to be with me any more

WOMAN
No
I want to be on my own
(*The MAN leaves. Quite long pause. The WOMAN and the FATHER OLDER look shyly towards each other, he then looks down, stands completely stiffly, with his eyes fixed down at an angle.*)
No
(*Pause.*)
Everyone who's been here
Everything that's happened
(*The WOMAN goes over and strokes the face of the FATHER OLDER.*)
And Father
Dear Father
I wish you'd lived longer
you sat there in the Seaman's home
and went out in the morning
for a few glasses of beer
then went back again
The days passed
they became
a few years
and then you were gone
Dear Father
(*Pause.*)
And I did come to visit you
in your room
at the Seaman's home
(*The FATHER OLDER goes out, and the MOTHER gets up from the sofa, walks out onto the floor, takes a position, resting on one leg and the UNCLE gets up, goes over to the MOTHER, unbuttons her blouse, takes it off, then he takes off*

his shirt, goes behind the MOTHER, holds her, first around the stomach, then her breasts, he touches her breasts and she leans against him, they kiss. The WOMAN stands watching, she becomes more and more embarassed; she becomes like a child in the face, and the GIRL looks towards the WOMAN, also embarassed, a bit giggly, then they both turn away but are curious, so they watch again, look down, not knowing quite what to do with themselves and the UNCLE presses the MOTHER into him, kisses her for a long time, then he loosens her skirt, it falls to the floor and the MOTHER is standing there in brown tights and the UNCLE fondles her bottom with both hands, they lie down on the floor, he lies on top of her.)

MOTHER

(*A little breathless.*)
But not
I'm not sure if
My daughters

UNCLE

They're not at home

MOTHER

(*Turns away.*)
Someone might come
(*The UNCLE lies on top of her again, kisses her, and then the FATHER walks in very slowly, he stops, looks towards the MOTHER and the UNCLE. Very long pause. The MOTHER sits up slowly. To the FATHER, scared.*)
Have you come
(*Pause.*)
home now
(*Pause.*)
then
(*Cuts herself off. The FATHER stands calmly and looks towards the MOTHER, who gets up while the UNCLE remains sitting on the floor. The FATHER just looks at them, then turns.*)
But

(*Pause.*)
is it you
or
you
I
are you here
But
(*The FATHER starts to leave slowly and the UNCLE gets up and the MOTHER looks at the FATHER leaving.*)
But
yes
I don't understand
(*Pause.*)
Are you going to leave again straight away
(*The FATHER leaves. Calls after him.*)
You've just arrived
so out of the blue
(*The UNCLE rebuttons his shirt.*)
I didn't know
But
you

WOMAN
(*Stands completely calm.*)
Father
It's so long since I've seen you
Where have you come from

GIRL
And you mustn't leave again
you mustn't leave straight away
Father
come back

WOMAN
Don't leave
I've been waiting for you
This is stupid

GIRL
You can't just leave

WOMAN
Father
Where are you
Don't say anything
(*Quite long pause. The WOMAN walks forward a little, looks towards the MOTHER and the UNCLE who stand looking uncomprehending towards each other. Pause.*)

UNCLE
It's not possible

MOTHER
It can't be real

UNCLE
He was just standing there all of a sudden

MOTHER
It's unbelievable
It's not possible
It's just stupid
(*The MOTHER laughs.*)

UNCLE
He came
He stood there
Like that
Just now
It happened just now

MOTHER
These things don't happen

UNCLE
Was he not
on a ship
some far away place or other

MOTHER
Yes
(*The MOTHER and the UNCLE look towards each other for a long time, then they laugh and then go out, first the MOTHER and then the UNCLE and at the same time the FATHER OLDER comes in.*)

WOMAN
And he never came back
Father never came back
He sent letters
(*The FATHER OLDER walks towards the WOMAN.*)
asked if he could meet me
my sister

WOMAN
(*To the FATHER OLDER.*)
Father
You just left

FATHER OLDER
I had to

WOMAN
You never saw Mother again

FATHER OLDER
I couldn't
I never wanted to see her
not after that
And I never did

WOMAN
You were never divorced

FATHER OLDER
I didn't want to see her

WOMAN
Never

FATHER OLDER
I never wanted to see her again
And I never saw her again

WOMAN
Now Mother's old
She's going to die

FATHER OLDER
I never wanted to see her again
(*The MOTHER comes in, in a dress suit, she stops, as if she is waiting for somebody to come, but nobody comes, she gets a little disappointed takes a position and stands as if in her own thoughts and then, after a while, the UNCLE enters and the FATHER OLDER goes out. Quite long pause.*)

SISTER OLDER
(*Comes in.*)
It's over
Mother's dead
She died tonight

WOMAN
Mother's dead

SISTER OLDER
She died tonight

WOMAN
She's dead

SISTER OLDER
It was going to happen
she'd been sick for a long time

WOMAN
No

SISTER OLDER
But now it's over

WOMAN
Were you there

SISTER OLDER
Yes
or
yes they rang
and I went as quickly as I could

WOMAN
Did you talk to her

SISTER OLDER
No
she couldn't talk
she just lay there
didn't say anything
just lay there

WOMAN
Did she

SISTER OLDER
Now she's dead
And we have to

WOMAN
(*Continues.*)
arrange the funeral

SISTER OLDER
I suppose we have to

WOMAN
Yes
(*The SISTER OLDER goes out, and the WOMAN looks towards the MOTHER who walks over to the UNCLE and leans into him, and he puts his arms around her, presses her towards him. The WOMAN looks away from them. To herself.*)
I tell myself that here is where we are
Here
Now
Just now
Just here

(*Short pause.*)
And here
(*Short pause.*)
here's where we're going to be
for quite a long time

GIRL
a very long time

WOMAN
incredibly long
(*Short pause.*)
or maybe not
maybe we aren't going to be here
(*Short pause.*)
but a totally different place
where it's quite different
(*Short pause.*)
I don't know

GIRL
I don't know anything

WOMAN
I don't know this
or anything else
or anything

GIRL
Nothing

WOMAN
Not a single thing in the world
Nothing
(*Short pause.*)
But it should be quiet
in the song
(*Thinks.*)
yes in the song
quiet

GIRL
so quiet

WOMAN
as quiet as an old day
(*Short pause.*)
So let it fade away
let it then come
let it then become
let it then be there
let it stay
let it stay there
let it stay there
and then
(*Cuts herself off. The WOMAN looks, takes a paintbrush and goes over to the picture of the girl on the sofa and paints across it, over it in black.*)
I can't paint
And I don't want to paint any more
(*Pause.*)
So now the girl on the sofa will have gone
(*The GIRL goes and sits in the corner of the sofa with her feet drawn up.*)
I can't paint things out
(*Quite short pause.*)
they're always there
Therefore I can't paint
(*Quite short pause. The WOMAN moves away from the picture and the MAN comes walking towards her and she walks towards him.*)

MAN
It was good to see you again

WOMAN
Yes
(*Short pause.*)
I just thought
it would be good to meet up

That's why I rang
It's been so long since last time

MAN
Yes it has been

WOMAN
You don't have to
meet me
if you don't want to
so

MAN
I'm alright now

WOMAN
Yes

MAN
We're happy together
Her and me

WOMAN
You and her
yes her
your new woman
you're happy together

MAN
Yes
(*Pause.*)
And you

WOMAN
Mother's dead

MAN
Yes I heard

WOMAN
Good to see you again

MAN

Yes it was good to see you
(*The WOMAN and the MAN look towards each other, then they walk away from each other.*)

WOMAN

(*After the MAN, who walks away and out.*)
But don't leave
Because then
(*Short pause.*)
because then
then I'll be completely alone
in the mornings
why should I get up

GIRL

I'm so alone
so alone that I haven't a face

WOMAN

I haven't a face
I can't see
there's not anything in me
to make me see
I don't have
(*Cuts herself off.*)

GIRL

I don't want to go out

WOMAN

And there's no-one else
only
(*Laughs briefly.*)
myself
and what's that
Something which sits here

GIRL

I'm not anything
just something which sits here

WOMAN

(*After the MAN, who has gone.*)
No don't go
No
because then
(*Cuts herself off. Pause.*)
No nothing
I can't do anything else
I haven't done anything else
And I'm not painting any more

SISTER

(*Comes in, wearing the net stockings, the patent leather skirt, high-heeled boots.*)
I'm going

GIRL

Where

SISTER

Out

GIRL

But where

SISTER

D'you have to know

GIRL

No
(*Pause.*)
Yes you just go
what're you waiting for

SISTER

I just thought I'd tell you

GIRL

Yes thanks

SISTER

D'you know where Mother is

GIRL
I've no idea

SISTER
D'you know what time she went out

GIRL
No

SISTER
Alright then

GIRL
You should go

SISTER
Yes I'm going
(*The WOMAN goes and sits in the right-hand corner of the sofa, also with her feet drawn up. The GIRL and the WOMAN look at each other.*)

Blackout.